Draw and color a picture of yourself inside the frame. Write your name on the lines below.

This is a picture of me. My name is

Write your age on the writing lines. Draw the correct number of candles on the cake. Color the picture.

I am _____ years old!

# Fill in the blanks and color the picture.

My birthday is on _____

On my next birthday, I will be _____ years old.

# Draw and color a picture of yourself when you were a baby.

Fill in the blanks.

My full name is

My mom's name is

My dad's name is

I was born in the year

# Draw and color a picture of you and your family.

# Write the first name and age of each person in your family.

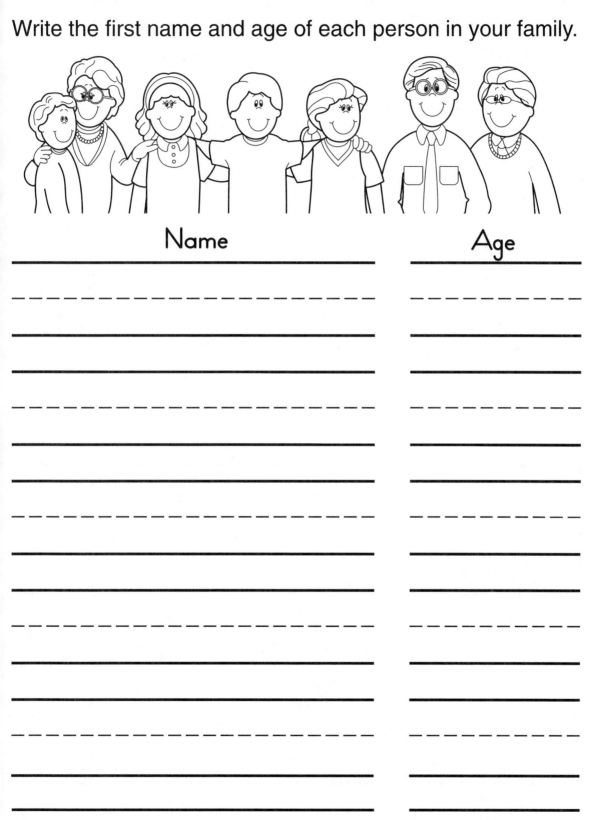

| Name | Age |
|------|-----|
|      |     |

Circle your favorite activity to do with your family. Color the pictures. If your favorite activity is not shown, draw it on the bottom of the next page.

# Draw and color a picture of your house.

Draw and color a picture of your bedroom. Write your favorite thing in your room on the lines below.

**My Room**

My favorite thing in my room is

_____

_ _ _ _ _ _ _ _ _ _ _ _ _ _ _ _ _ _ _ _ _ _ _ _ _

.

_____

_____

Write your name and address on the writing lines.

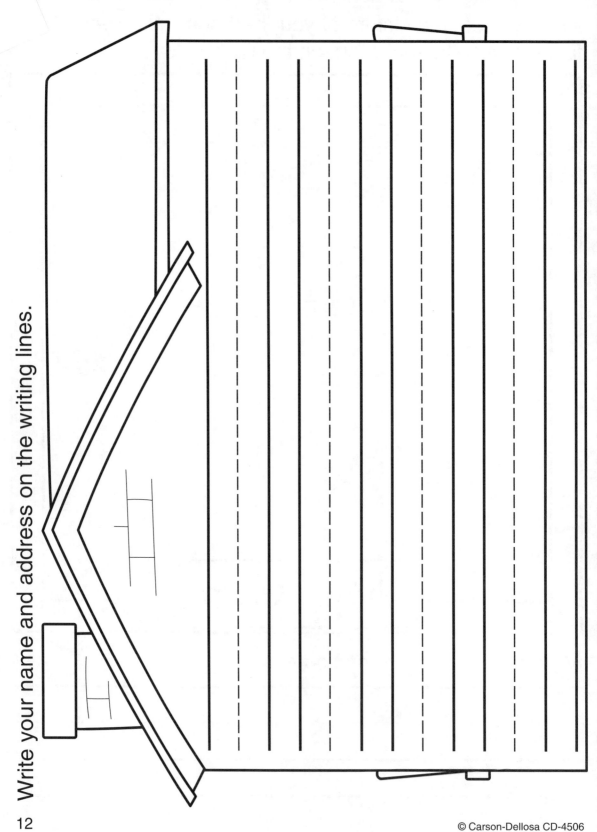

12

Write your answers on the writing lines.

My phone number is

_____

- - - - - - - - - - - - - - - - - - - - - - - - - -

_____ .

When I answer the phone, I say

_____

- - - - - - - - - - - - - - - - - - - - - - - - - -

_____ .

_____

Trace and write this number to call in an emergency.

911

Circle the things that make you smile. Color the pictures. At the bottom of the next page, draw something that makes you laugh.

14

1,001
Knock-Knock
Jokes

Look at the first picture in each row. Circle the face that shows how the first picture might make you feel. Color the pictures.

Look at the first picture in each row. Circle the face that shows how the first picture might make you feel. Color the pictures.

# Draw a picture of yourself doing one of your favorite things.

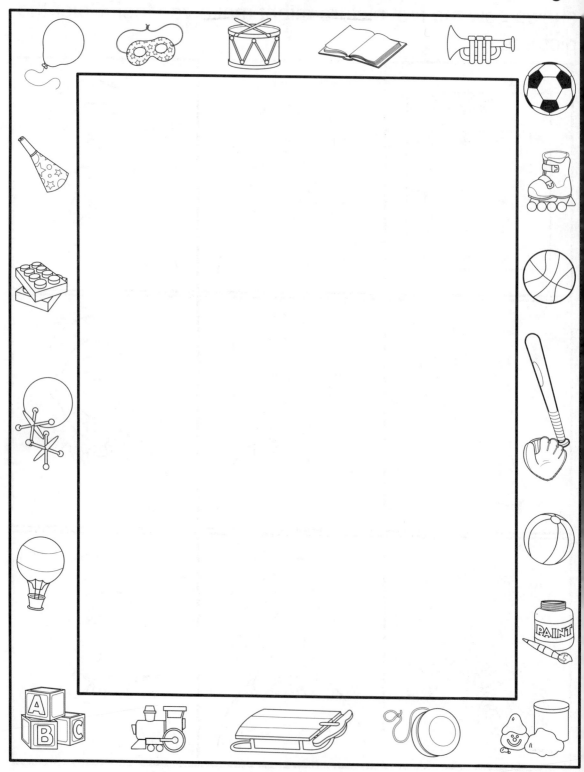

Circle your favorite place to be. Color the pictures. If your favorite place is not shown, draw and color it in the box below.

Draw and color a picture of your pet or your favorite animal. Write its name on the lines below.

The name of my pet or favorite animal is

_____

– – – – – – – – – – – – – – – – – – – – – – – –

_____

_____

Draw and color a picture inside the treasure chest of something that you treasure or is very special to you.

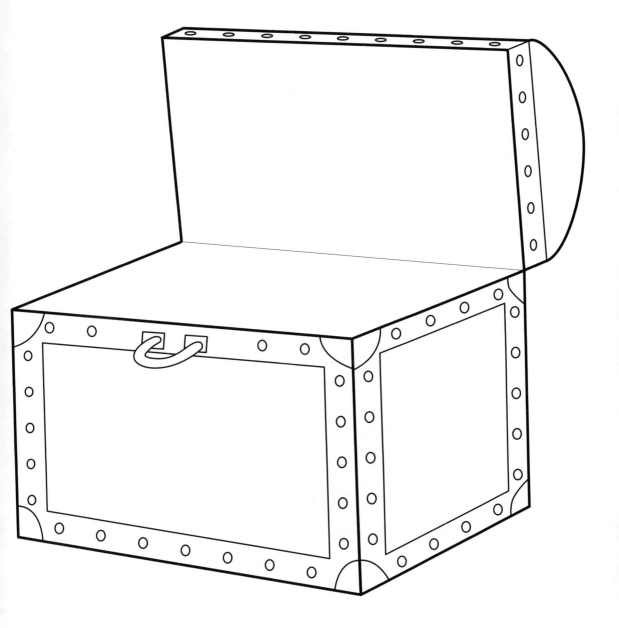

Color each crayon the correct color. Write the name of your favorite color on the lines below.

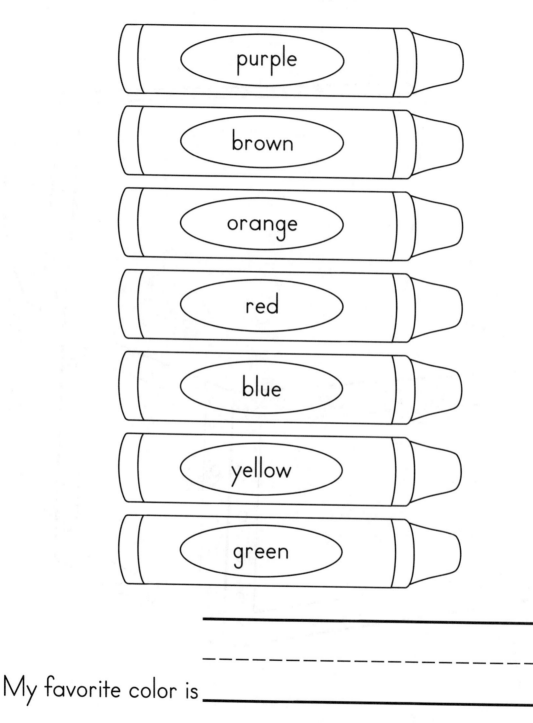

My favorite color is _____.

Circle the pictures that are colors you like. Draw and color a picture of something that is your favorite color.

# Draw and color a picture of yourself in your favorite clothes.

Draw and color a picture inside the toy box of your favorite toy. Write the name of the toy on the lines below.

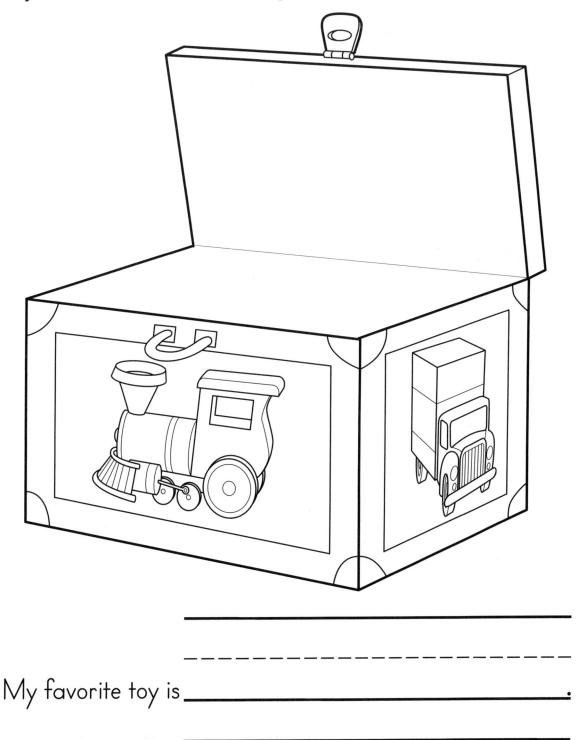

My favorite toy is _____.

Draw and color your favorite food on the plate. Write the name of the food on the lines below.

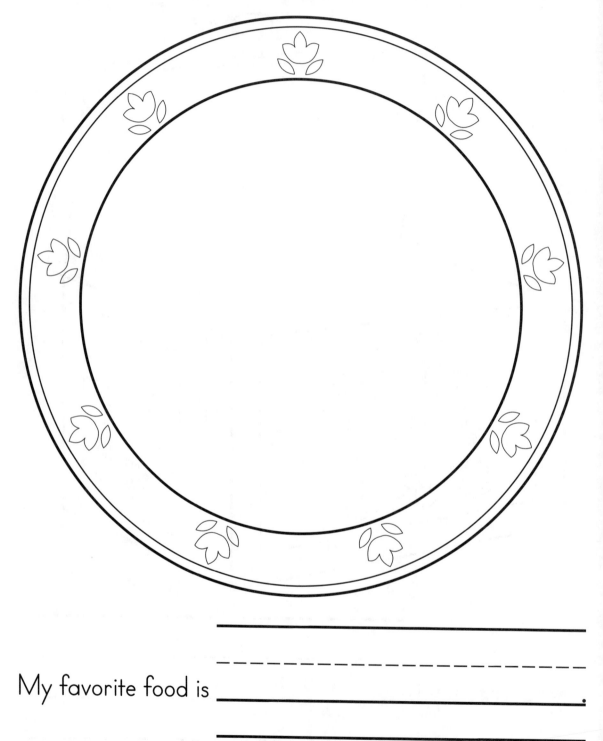

My favorite food is _____.

Circle your favorite dessert. Color the pictures. If your favorite dessert is not shown, draw and color it in the box below.

# Color the fruits and vegetables that you like to eat.

Draw and color a picture of your favorite thing to drink.
Write the name of the drink on the lines below.

My favorite drink is _____.

Write the title of your favorite book. Then, draw and color a scene from the book.

My favorite book is _____

_____

_____.

_____

Draw and color the characters from your favorite movie.
Write the name of the movie on the lines below.

_____

_ _ _ _ _ _ _ _ _ _ _ _ _ _ _ _ _ _

My favorite movie is _____

_____

_ _ _ _ _ _ _ _ _ _ _ _ _ _ _ _ _ _ _ _ _ _

_____ .

_____

# Color the picture that shows your favorite time of year.

Put the scenes in the correct order. Write 1, 2, 3, or 4 in the box in the corner of each scene.

Circle the picture that shows your favorite holiday. Draw and color a picture of your favorite holiday below if it is not shown.

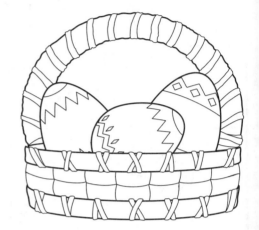

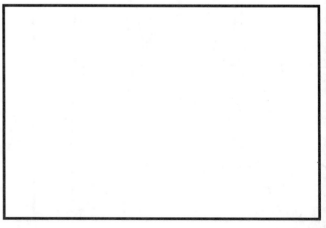

# Draw and color you and your family celebrating your favorite holiday. Write the name of the holiday on the lines below.

My favorite holiday is

_____

_ _ _ _ _ _ _ _ _ _ _ _ _ _ _ _ _ _ _ _ _ _ _ _ _

_____

_____

# Circle the picture that shows your favorite type of weather. Color the pictures.

Circle the picture that shows what you wear in your favorite type of weather. Color the pictures.

Circle the picture that shows your favorite game or sport. Color the pictures. Write the name of your favorite game on the bottom of the next page.

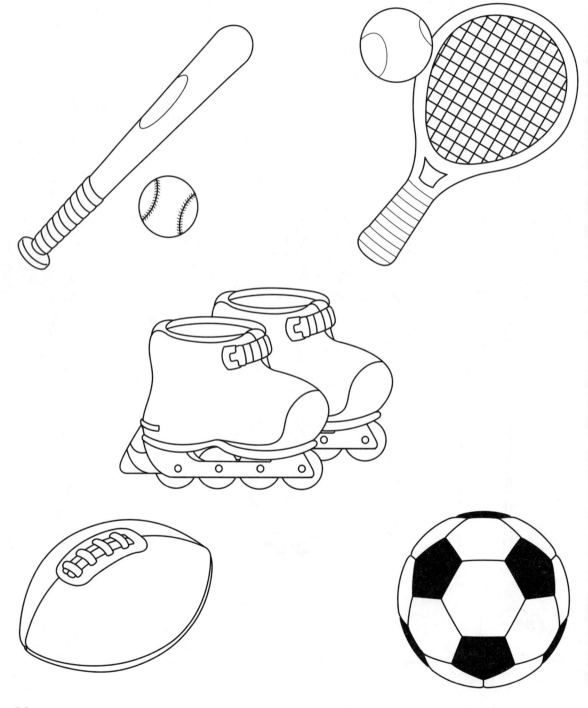

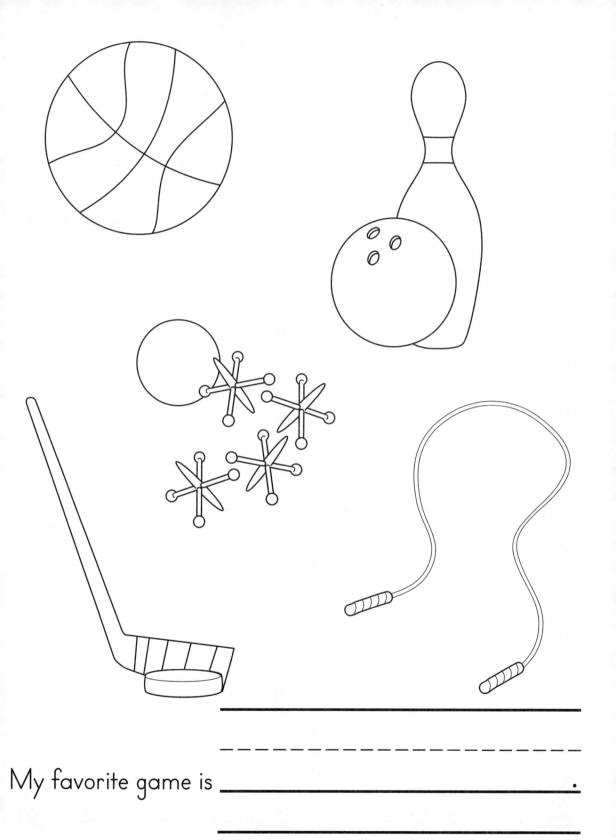

My favorite game is _____.

Write the name of your favorite place to take a trip. Draw and color pictures of things you saw on your trip.

_____

- - - - - - - - - - - - - - - - - - - - - - - - -

My trip to _____ was fun!

_____

Draw and color a picture of a place you would like to visit someday. Write the name of the place on the lines below.

I would like to visit

_____

_____ .

_____

Draw and color a picture of two of your friends. Write their names on the lines below.

My friends' names are _____

and _____.

Circle the things you like to do with your friends. Color the pictures. If your favorite thing to do is not shown, draw a picture of it in the box below.

# Draw and color a picture of your school.

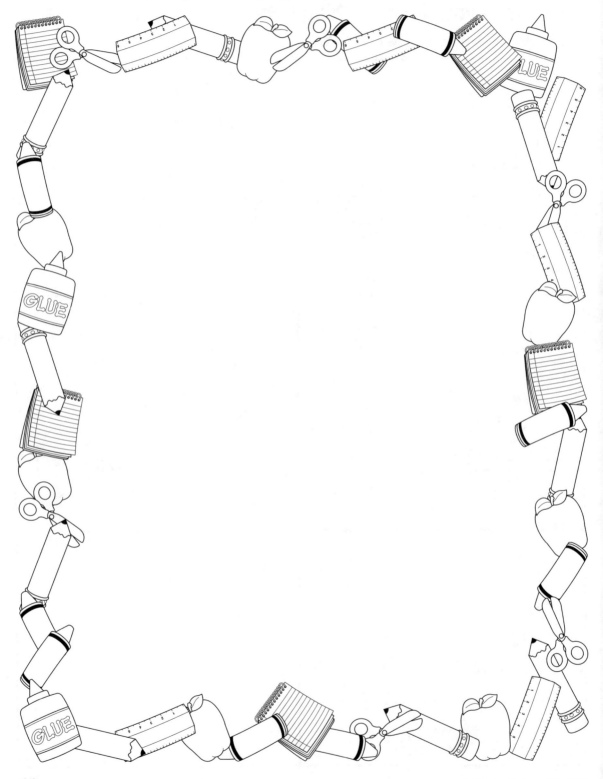

44

**Fill in the blanks about your school.**

The name of my school is

_____

- - - - - - - - - - - - - - - - - - - - - - - - - - - - - - - - - - - -

_____.

_____

I am in grade _____

- - - - - - - - - - - - - - - - - - - - - - - - - - - - - - - - - - - -

_____.

_____

My teacher's name is _____

- - - - - - - - - - - - - - - - - - - - - - - - - - - - - - - - - - - -

_____.

_____

My favorite thing to do at school is _____

- - - - - - - - - - - - - - - - - - - - - - - - - - - - - - - - - - - -

_____

_____

- - - - - - - - - - - - - - - - - - - - - - - - - - - - - - - - - - - -

_____.

_____

On this page and the next, circle the things that you are able to do. Color the pictures.

Draw and color a picture of yourself doing something that you do well.

Draw and color a picture of what you would like to learn to do someday. Write your answer on the lines below.

Someday, I would like to learn how to

_____

— — — — — — — — — — — — — — — — — — — — — —

_____ .

# You can trace the alphabet! Trace each uppercase letter.

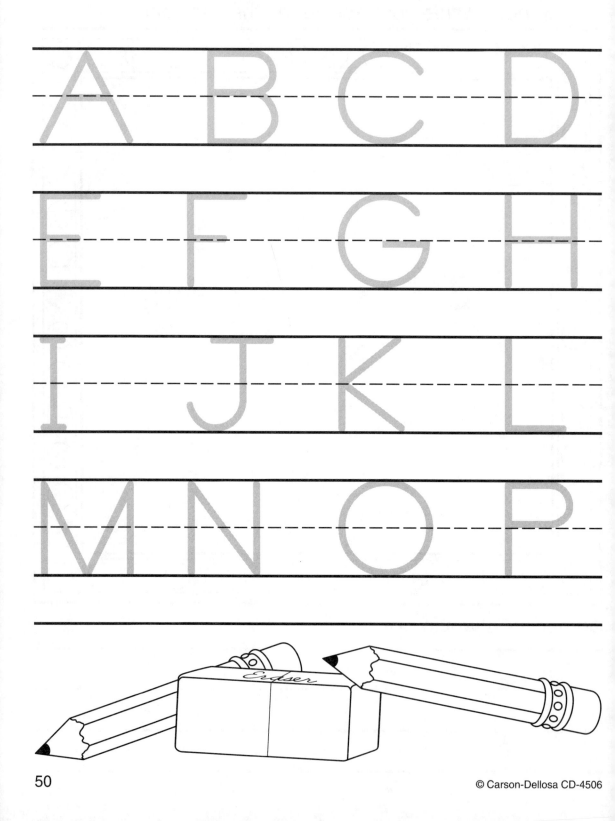

Fill in the blanks to record how big you are today.

Today's date is

_____

- - - - - - - - - - - - - - - - - - - - - - - - - - - -

_____ .

_____

I am this tall.

- - - - - - - - - - - - - - - - - - - - - - -

_____

_____

I weigh this much.

- - - - - - - - - - - - - - - - - - - - - - -

_____

Color the pictures of the things you do to stay healthy.

# Trace and color your hand.

This is my hand.

Draw and color what you think you will look like when you are grown.

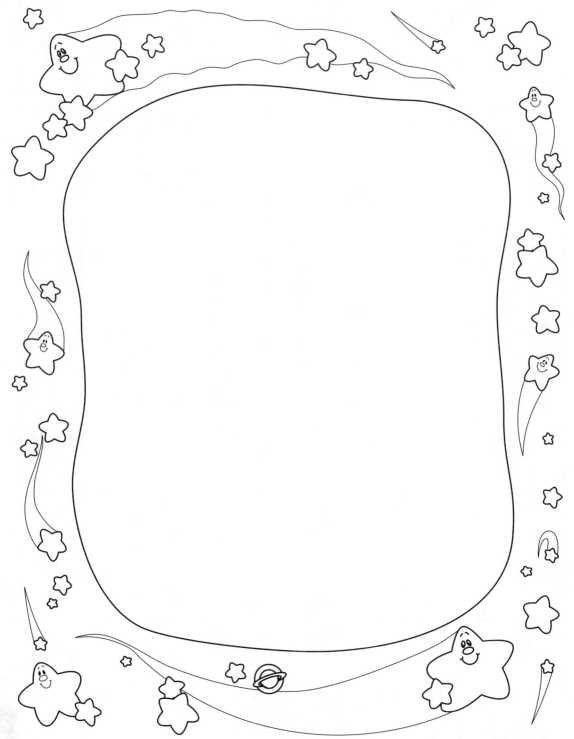

Draw and color what you think your house or neighborhood will look like when you are grown.

Circle the picture of what you would like to be when you grow up. Draw a picture on the bottom of the next page if your choice is not shown.

Draw and color a picture of what you think and dream about. Write your thoughts on the lines below.

Color the pictures that show things you do every day to stay healthy. Draw another way you stay healthy below.

Ask your family and friends to sign their names and write messages to you.

# Autographs